Family Business

*Genesis 37 - 50
and the Family of Joseph*

Also by Lance Woodbury

The Enduring Legacy: Essential Family Business Values

Also by William R. Long

Everyone's Angry: Homer's Iliad, Book One
Word Wealth: 300 Words for Pleasure and Profit
It's All the Basics: Teaching and Learning for the 21st Century
Wisdom Seeking: Thirty Days with the Book of Proverbs
52 and Strangely Found
A Hard Fought Hope: Journeying with Job Through Mystery
A Tortured History: The Story of Capital Punishment in Oregon
Yearning Minds and Burning Hearts: Rediscovering the Spirituality of Jesus
Who in the World Can You Trust?
Called to Serve: A Curriculum for Church Leaders
Out of Darkness: The Story of Shawn Huff
Trusting God Again: Regaining Hope after Disappointment or Loss
Longing for God: Prayer and the Rhythms of Life
39 and Lost in America

Family Business

*Genesis 37 - 50
and the Family of Joseph*

Lance Woodbury

William R. Long

COPYRIGHT © 2013 Lance D. Woodbury
William R. Long

ALL RIGHTS RESERVED

Cover Art: Gustave Doré, Joseph Reveals Himself to His Brothers
Picture from The Holy Scriptures, Old and New Testaments books collection published in 1885, Stuttgart-Germany

Cover and Book Design by Jerri Strozier

ISBN: 978-1493502479

No part of this book may be used or reproduced in any form or by any means, electronic or mechanical, without written permission from the author, except for the inclusion of brief quotations in a review.

Additional resources at
www.lancewoodbury.com

For Terry Woodbury
Father and Friend
Skillful Weaver of Faith and Life

Table of Contents

Introduction 9

1: The Backstory of the Story 13

2: Favorites, Egos & Jockeying for Power 21

3: Payback Time! 29

4: When Temptation Comes 37

5: Ignored! 45

6: The Conflict Deepens 53

7: Desperation All Around 61

8: On the Precarious Edge 69

9: Found Out! 75

10: Reconciliation At Last! 81

11: Blessing the Children 89

12: Making Reconciliation Last 97

Introduction

FAMILIES AND BUSINESSES are two of the more complex organizations in our society. When the two concepts or entities are married, becoming a "family business," the complexities of the resultant organization multiply. Complementing the difficulties of establishing and maintaining a viable and profitable business enterprise are the richly textured, and sometimes impossible to manage, relationships among employees or family members that may reach back several generations. Opportunities for both enormous satisfaction and debilitating and corrosive interactions are legion.

This book is unique among family business books in that it attempts to explore some of the vast array of dynamics in families and families-in-business through a systematic study of the Biblical story of the family of Joseph (Genesis 37-50). Like a huge spotlight illuminating a dark corner of our lives, the Joseph story probes with skill the range of emotions and actions that family members feel and take towards each other in both the good and stressful times of family life.

The following list is only a partial compilation of the family dynamics we meet in the Joseph story: current-day conflicts that originated in earlier generations, sibling rivalry, parental favoritism, jealousy, payback strategies towards "unruly" family members, what "fairness" looks like, sexual temptation and even violence, when to speak and when to listen, responding to dismal economic times, reconciliation after repeated family crises, passing a (mixed) heritage to the next generation.

As we read these stories, two themes emerge time and again. First are the genuine *tensions* or *ambiguities* experienced by family members as they deal with the complexities of familial and business life and the realization that there often are no easy answers to tough and insistent questions. For example, there is no easy answer to how one should deal with an overbearing brother. Or with the feeling of vulnerability brought upon a family by economic crisis. Or with the despair felt by parents convinced they have lost a child, either figuratively or literally. Second, however, is the sense that behind the family narrative—behind the history, the drama and the chaos—is the operation of a faithful God, a God whose influence is apparent, even if it cannot always be felt.

How to Use This Book

We try to explore all these themes, and more, in this book. We divide each chapter into three parts: an exposition of an engaging Biblical passage in the Joseph story that illustrates dynamics of families and families in business; a "modern" reading of the passage with special focus on the way the passage helps us frame issues faced in real-life family business contexts; and a few searching questions that show how to use the Biblical story and our modern reading of it in your own family/family business. Our perspective throughout is that a close and nuanced reading of the Bible story helps us identify and faithfully deal with a range of issues that confront us as family members and, often, members of a family business.

We hope you will use this book not only as a personal guide to an engaging Biblical story but also as a catalyst for engaged family discussions on the themes we raise. We hope that you will try carefully to answer the questions we raise and that, as a result, your family and family business will be strengthened.

The Authors

This is a collaborative effort of two friends who have known each other since Lance was a student in Bill's classrooms at Sterling College in Kansas in the early 1990s. Bill brings to this task a wealth of experience in making the message of the Bible alive to lay people and pastors. Some of his previous books have been on the Psalms, Jesus, Job and, most recently, the Book of Proverbs. Lance has, since finishing Sterling College and a pair of Masters Degree programs, been both an executive with a prominent Midwest consulting and accounting firm and a noted family business consultant. His previous book, *The Enduring Legacy: Essential Family Business Values* (2012), has received widespread and favorable comment.

We invite you to engage in the fascinating journey of using the Biblical story as a teaching and listening tool that opens the pulsating realities of our own world in a fresh and effective way.

Chapter One

The Backstory of the Story
(Gen. 25:24-28)

"When her (Rebekah's) time to give birth was at hand, there were twins in her womb. The first came out red, all his body like a hairy mantle; so they named him Esau. Afterward his brother came out, with his hand gripping Esau's heel; so he was named Jacob...When the boys grew up, Esau was a skillful hunter, a man of the field, while Jacob was a quiet man, living in tents. Isaac loved Esau, because he was fond of game; but Rebekah loved Jacob."

AS WE MEET the FAMILY of Joseph, we realize that the problems of his generation that will occupy us in this book don't originate in his generation. They were there in some form with his parents (Jacob, Rachel) and even his grandparents. The Psalmist might say about his life: "The lines have fallen for me in pleasant places; I have a goodly heritage" (Ps. 16:6), and that certainly is true, but we have to consider that intergenerational conflicts are also part of our familial DNA.

In this case, the family of divine promise is the family of diverse problems. The covenant family is the conflicted family. To make matters worse, it isn't really clear exactly how the conflict in the family emerged or whether it has any realistic solution. Sometimes conflict just "is," and the only thing you can do is to try to manage the fallout. In this chapter we will explore the way that conflict in previous generations sets the tone for the current generation's life.

Conflict's Mysterious Origin

If Joseph had asked his father Jacob about the origin of some of the family problems, Jacob could have pointed to many things. Perhaps it was an unequal land distribution between the brothers; perhaps it was Jacob's bald attempt to deprive Esau of his inheritance, perhaps something else. But, as we read these verses, we are plunged into a deeper mystery. Perhaps no one really can put his finger on the origin of the conflict. Or, more precisely, are we meant to understand that Jacob's gripping his brother's heel in the womb already indicates a pre-conscious attempt to upstage his brother, a pre-birth way to supplant him? But attractive as that interpretation is at first glance, it really doesn't match our life experience. We just don't "blame" infants for initiating family conflicts. Or, if we do, we are being blind to the real dynamics behind conflict. So, here we are treated to a mystery. Conflict seems to emerge in a time before we can assign responsibility.

Different Genetic Makeup

The Bible doesn't use a phrase that is a staple of our current-day conversation. In our day, when asked why someone is like she is, we often say, "Well, it is in the genes." And we know immediately what the other person means. So, it seems that Esau and Jacob had a different genetic makeup or, less pointedly, different personal inclinations. One liked "guy" things, hunting and the challenge of the chase. One liked domestic things, the quiet life of the tents. Who is to explain why the brothers are different? We all know that sibling difference is as common as winter cold, but somehow we often still have trouble dealing with it.

Different Parental Loves

Most parents, when asked about their affection for their children, invariably say, "I love them all the same." Some more honest parents might say, "I love them all the same, but one of them really is like their mother/father, while one takes after me." Yet, the issue of parceling out affection based on interest, based on children's inclinations and love, is a tender and difficult subject. Where does one parent's "love" for one child because of similarity to the parent become a form of favoritism? Even if it is not so intended by the parents, who say, "I love them all equally," what about if different treatment is *experienced* by the children as favoritism? What lessons do children learn because "Rebekah loved Jacob," but "Isaac loved Esau"? As the backstory develops, we see each of the two brothers developing his own personality. Esau is impulsive and aggressive, often acting heedless of consequences. Jacob skillfully perceives vulnerabilities in others and knows how to exploit these vulnerabilities. But we can't forget that this is the family through which God has chosen to act. These are the people of God, the family of promise, the individuals of blessing. These are the ones that will bequeath to Joseph and his brothers not simply the skills and passion of life, but also many of the tensions that rip apart a later generation.

Reflection and Questions

✍ Reflection One: Every Family is Imperfect

I remember my childhood days when my grandmother, after a particularly difficult family conflict, would sigh and say, "Why can't we be like the Thomas family up the road? They are such a perfect family. They just don't have *any* problems!" Even though

I was young, I remember saying to her, "Grandma, they have their issues too, but they just do a better job of hiding them!"

Family problems have been with us forever, though only in the 1980s did family counselors and psychologists start using the words "dysfunction" or "dysfunctional" to describe family dynamics. The language caught on like wildfire. You probably recall that everyone, from solemn clergy to giddy teenagers rolling their eyes, would say of people, "'X' has *such* a dysfunctional family." After being a family business consultant for nearly two decades, I can chime in and say, in slightly different words, "Imperfection is inherent in every family's life."

And we see this imperfection writ large in one of the best-known family stories in the Bible. The family is indeed "normal," with the differences between Jacob and Esau, the inclination of each parent toward a particular child, and the anticipated rivalry – and that is before the story gets good! When you bring different personalities together, living in close proximity over a long period of time, working together day in and day out, the fault lines are bound to emerge. People will gravitate toward one another in certain alliances. People will do a poor job of communicating with one another. People will get frustrated. To pretend that doesn't happen is to deny what we fundamentally know about humans living and working together.

The question therefore is not whether family imperfection exists. The question is how the family will deal with it. Does the family admit it? Or does the family try to bottle it up, pretending that everything is perfect or, if not perfect, easily under control? So many times in the Bible, we see that God has chosen an improbable, imperfect person to communicate His message. In this case it is an imperfect family, with all the issues that plague any modern family today, that carries God's message.

Questions for Reflection and Discussion:

What is one area in which your family is less than perfect?

Do people in your family admit to this imperfection? Try to ignore it or cover it up?

Has there ever been an attempt in your family to talk about these difficult issues? What have been the results?

Does your family have any kind of agreement, written or unwritten, that people need to work together to get through the difficult times?

✍ Reflection Two: Inheriting Conflict

Families with financial assets and operating businesses are rightly concerned with passing of such wealth and management perspectives to future generations. Taxes, divorce, creditors, business volatility and other factors are the reasons families conduct extensive planning with accountants, attorneys, financial advisors and insurance agents.

Too often, however, the family may keep the wealth intact but ruin the relationships required to hold it together for another generation. Consider this: if two brothers working in a closely held business are having problems with one another, and their young children pick up on the tension between the two – or overhear their parents talking about how frustrated they are – what do you think happens between the cousins?

I know such a situation. Two brothers, now in their 60s, had a divisive and bitter argument 30 years ago regarding farming methods in adjoining parcels owned by the family. The conflict became so severe that voices were raised, threats were issued and the brothers almost came to blows. Their young children didn't witness the fight, but from that day forward ended up seeing little of their cousins. Thirty years later, these "children" have grown up and have families of their own. They still live in the same town, but rarely see each other. It is as if they live in different countries or speak different languages. No one yet has tried to unravel the complexities of the fallout. One thing is clear, however. The conflict of a generation ago is still "alive and well" today.

Questions for Discussion

Has there been any conflict or a split from previous generations that is still "alive" in your family or family business history?

What was the effect of these conflicts or splits on the next generation's relationships?

If you measured your family business relationships on a scale of 1-10, with 1 being good and 10 being poor, how would you "score" them?

When you think about other partners in the family business, is your opinion of them influenced by what you know of their backstory, i.e., the previous generations of their family?

Chapter Two

Favorites, Egos & Jockeying for Power
(Gen. 37:2-4)

"This is the story of the family of Jacob. Joseph, being seventeen years old, was shepherding the flock with his brothers; he was a helper to the sons of Bilhah and Zilpah, his father's wives; and Joseph brought a bad report of them to their father. Now Israel (Jacob) loved Joseph more than any other of his children, because he was the son of his old age; and he made him a long robe with sleeves. But when his brothers saw that their father loved him more than all his brothers, they hated him, and could not speak peaceably to him."

THIS STORY PLUNGES us into the middle of a collapsing family system and family business. The simplicity of the narrative belies an enormously complex family dynamic. Jacob had 12 sons, by four different women: Leah, Bilhah, Zilpah and Rachel. If that isn't enough, he favored the first son of his beloved Rachel by making him an ornate robe (the "coat of many colors" in the King James Version). This gift, no doubt motivated by love, became a hated symbol of favoritism, a sign of inequality, a constant and gnawing reminder to the older sons that they weren't quite as "good" as the favored son.

To make matters worse, Joseph rubbed their nose in it. He brought a "bad report" to his father about his brothers. He was undermining them. Then, as the narrative goes on, it tells of two dreams Joseph had, in which all his brothers and even his father would soon be bowing down and serving him. The closing words of this chapter's Biblical passage say it all, "they (the brothers) hated him, and could not speak peaceably to him."

The story challenges us today, and especially those who are trying to have children get along with each other in the management of family affairs. First, as we saw in the previous chapter, family dynamics were significantly compromised *before* any of the brothers had anything to do with it. All of this goes back yet before the present generation, to Jacob and his brother Esau and then, behind that, to his parents Isaac and Rebekah. We have a multi-generational crisis that will come to a head with the colorful robe and the twelve brothers.

Second, a parent's misjudgment can contribute enormous anguish and ill-will to family business dynamics. In this case we have the clear example of favoritism through the making of a robe for Joseph. But in fact, isn't it very difficult to treat all children *equally*? Does equal treatment mean that everyone gets exactly the same share or portion of everything? Perhaps Jacob not only loved his son Joseph but perceived in him certain qualities that set him apart from the others—qualities that would assure the success of the family and its vast business operations.

Third, favoritism often leads to jockeying for position, as egos of various strength are pitted against each other while the sons try to earn parental approval or even undermine each other. Joseph had a dream, which was his way of trying to "jockey" for position in the family. Listen to the following words:

"Once Joseph had a dream, and when he told it to his brothers, they hated him even more. He said to them, 'Listen to this dream that I dreamed. There we were, binding sheaves in the field. Suddenly my sheaf rose and stood upright; then your sheaves gathered round it, and bowed down to my sheaf.' His brothers said to him, 'Are you indeed to reign over us?'...So they hated him even more because of his dreams and his words," (Gen. 37:5-8).

Joseph is already trying to "pull rank" on his older brothers. After all, he could argue that his dream was from God, that it was clear in its meaning and that it ought to be honored. But, perhaps the favoritism of his father made him blind to the effect that his action had on his brothers. Joseph obviously felt no qualms about sharing the specifics of his dream with his brothers. In a word he is saying, 'Not only does my father favor me more than you, but the dream does, too.' Who *wouldn't* hate such a brother?

So, in the very beginning of a 14-chapter family story, we have all the makings of a huge blowup, a disaster of immense proportions. The natural one to "solve" the problem, Jacob, is compromised and unreliable. The sons are either nursing their wounds, planning for retaliation or, in the case of Joseph, preening himself for his eventual 'inheritance' of the family mantel. The Scriptures don't sugar-coat it. The family is in trouble.

Reflection and Questions

✍ Reflection One: Fairness, Equality and Treating Children Differently

From a family business perspective, this story – early in its telling – shares much with modern family businesses. The most obvious is the unhealthy balance between Jacob and his children. Clearly Joseph was his favorite, and Jacob made no bones about it. He saw Joseph's strengths, but the way he recognized Joseph's strengths probably bolstered a prideful attitude in Joseph. The other brothers are not singled out in any positive way; thus Jacob's expression of favor, symbolized in a coat, comes at the expense of the other brothers.

We often say in family business that "fair is not equal," meaning that people should be treated differently, just as Joseph was. The trick is not to let this difference show up as favoritism. In other words, if "fair" should not be "equal," then "different" should not be "favorite." But that is easier said than done in the family business.

Signs of treating siblings differently in a family are legion. Sometimes it is an heirloom gift, but more often in a family business it comes in the form of financial assistance or forgiveness, of asset purchases, or in time spent with certain family members and not others. Sometimes this kind of conduct is reflected in the favorable treatment of sons over daughters, or of those who stayed in the business versus those who chose not to return, or of those who chose certain career paths or even spouses. Even if parents might forget how much time and money they spend on individual children, the children never forget.

Questions for Reflection and Discussion:

Did your parents treat you differently than your siblings? How so? Do you agree that this different treatment was good, or were there negative features to it?

Did your parents do a good job of balancing fairness and favoritism?

Would your children recognize favoritism in your behavior toward them? If so, what repercussions might this perception have on the business?

✍ Reflection Two: Family Member Strengths and Your Impact on Others

In any organization – especially a family business – it is important to recognize that each family member has strengths, a unique ability to affect the world in a certain way. That distinct contribution does not always find a place in the family business, but as parents our job is to recognize and support those unique attributes. If we focus only – or too heavily – on the gifts of one, we set up dysfunctional relationships with our other children and foster an unhealthy relationship between them. By doing this, it is as if we put an invisible wedge between those most important to us, and thus we sow the seeds of divisiveness that haunt us later in life.

What is often the case, however, is that a family member's unique strength often turns into occasions for conflict. In this case, Joseph seems unaware of his impact on his brothers. While the dream of his brothers bowing before him indeed came true as the story develops, his sharing the dream with his siblings reminds me of how often one sibling is unaware of the impact they have on other siblings. For example, in one business where I consulted, one of the brothers continually talked about his efforts, never recognized anyone else's work, and, even though he was recognized by others for his skills, insisted on continually being affirmed for everything he did. He never realized why people gradually withdrew from working with him and why the family business suffered as a result.

In another business, one of the sisters publicly criticized how the family spent money. Rather than leading to understanding, this actually led to her being cut out of the "spending loop" in the family business, to her chagrin and the family's eventual anguish. She never realized that had she gently raised questions about spending, all might have been different. Finally, I have seen situations where one sibling's lack of planning and his impulsive action ended up creating chaos in the business and family relationships; all the time he was unaware that he was causing the problems.

Such people could be the smartest, the handiest, or most business-savvy team member, but they simply drive everyone around them crazy. The "obnoxious and bothersome brother" or "uncaring and selfish sister" brings negativity to both business transactions and family events with remarkable consistency. Family members whisper or talk afterwards about how much their brother or sister dampens the interaction, but they are unable to help that family member see the error in his or her ways.

Joseph, too, created a hostile environment with his brothers, and he was seemingly unaware that he was doing it.

Questions for Reflection and Discussion:

Whom do you know in other family businesses (or your own) that has a negative effect on others? What specifically do they do to provoke this negative feeling?

How do you deal with people who seem unaware of the negative effect they have on a family or family business?

Do your family members see you as a contributor or detractor to the cohesiveness of the organization?

Is your impact on other family members what you want it to be?

Chapter Three

Payback Time!

(Gen. 37:17-20)

"So Joseph went after his brothers, and found them at Dothan. They saw him from a distance, and before he came near to them, they conspired to kill him. They said to one another, 'Here comes this dreamer. Come now, let us kill him and throw him into one of the pits; then we shall say that a wild animal has devoured him, and we shall see what will become of his dreams.'"

LAST TIME WE saw the corrosive effects of unhealthy family dynamics: parental favoritism, one brother undermining the others, and narcissistic dreaming. Jacob's poor judgment, in making the ornate coat for Joseph, made the other sons seethe with anger. Three times in five verses the story tells us that they "hated him," or they "hated him even more" or "they hated him all the more." Bad, worse, worst. Simple, comparative, superlative. We get the message. Barely controlled anger among the brothers.

To make matters worse, the brothers couldn't really do anything to retaliate. Joseph was under the protective wing of his father Jacob. The brothers had to be content with nurturing their rage and looking for an opportunity to retaliate against their brother. Interestingly enough, as we will see below, the brothers appear to be united when they have the common enemy in their brother; as soon as they remove him from their midst, their own hidden conflicts come to the surface. The family is a gurgling laboratory of discontent.

Payback Strategies

Finally the opportunity for payback comes! The irony is that it comes through Jacob's miscalculation. Just as he misjudged the effect of the colorful coat, so he misjudges the situation again. How? He sends his son Joseph out to "check on" his brothers again, this time while the brothers were far removed from the protective shield of Joseph (v. 14). Joseph, wrapped up in his own narcissistic fantasies, can't see the writing on the wall. He is in danger and doesn't know it.

The brothers realize their big chance has come. Now, they can get rid of their brother once for all! Difficulties begin to arise because the brothers develop three different possible payback strategies:

1) Perhaps they should kill him and throw his body in a pit, reporting back to Jacob that a wild beast had devoured Joseph. They no doubt would report the news with tears streaming down their cheeks.
2) Reuben, the oldest, got squeamish with this idea and suggested that they should just throw him in the pit and let nature take its course. But Reuben had ulterior motives. He wanted to return to the crime scene, save his brother, restore him to Joseph and receive a proper reward. Reuben knew that his father played favorites. Why not try to become one now?

3) Finally, Judah suggested that they sell Joseph to passing traders. The brothers agreed, and they did so. This may have assuaged the brothers' guilt, but it presented them with another set of problems. How do you explain the disappearance of Joseph to father Jacob? And, furthermore, what do you do with the money? You could play dumb. "Huh, you mean Joseph? Huh, never saw him." But affected stupidity both then and now usually doesn't win in the end. Someone is going to blow your cover.

It is hard to keep a conspiracy completely quiet, especially when you have as many as 10 brothers implicated in the crime, money is involved, and ambition exists to try to curry favor with the father. I could imagine that Reuben was already developing a strategy to betray his brothers perhaps by leaking some information to his father and blaming the others for the disappearance, with the goal of becoming the "replacement" son for Joseph in his father's affection.

Results

The Scriptures never tell us the interior musings or thoughts of the brothers in the wake of this act of retribution. Though we might characterize it as both violent and criminal, we understand it completely. By doing it, the brothers will excise this cancer from their midst. Radical surgery, but with no chemo. No radiation. The hoped result: complete and immediate remission.

But life and family dynamics don't work that way. You can't just lop people off and expect to solve your problem. Anything might happen. Even things you don't imagine....

Reflection and Questions

꧁ Reflection One: How to Get Rid of a Family Member

Joseph's brothers worked on a number of strategies to "eliminate" him as the problem. And they landed on one—sell him. Problem solved. And why shouldn't it be? When thinking of employees, we often say that as employers we should be "slow to hire, fast to fire," reinforcing the notion that firing ends the relationship. We have contracts and employment agreements all designed to sever the connection. You get the ex-employee's keys, allow them to gather their things, and wish them well.

But in family business, when you "fire" a family member, they usually are not gone. They may no longer be active in the daily management system. You may even have a buy-sell agreement to purchase their ownership. But that family member is still – and probably forever – in the family system: the web of relationships that comprise our deepest and most historical connections to one another. The relationship has indeed changed, but it is far from over. Funerals, anniversaries, birthdays, sibling and cousin relationships, grandparent relationships…there are all kinds of reasons that will likely require at least some minimal interaction between family members, regardless if they work together.

Being in a family business, or heirs to family assets, often calls us back to interacting with one another legally and financially as the complexity of family business ownership and estate planning are managed. In one case I worked with, the family stopped interacting socially and even split part of the family farming business to get rid of a troublesome sibling, only to have the grandparents "skip" a generation with a gift of land in their estate plan, thus putting the expelled sibling right back into a key owner role. Oops.

If you try to eliminate siblings, the impact from the cut-off is far-reaching. From cousins not liking each other, to grandparents being held at arms length from their grandkids, the act of disconnecting usually impacts a far broader group than those directly involved in conflict. Family members may be out of sight for some period of time, but perhaps because of our early love for family members or our desire to be in a bonded relationship, they are never out of mind.

Questions for Reflection and Discussion:

Do you know of situations where people have been cut off in family business?

What has been the result when you've tried to simply disconnect from a family member?

✐ Reflection Two: Your Decisions Have Consequences

Another reflection from this passage is that families should be mindful that their decisions often have significant consequences. When Jacob decided to send Joseph to find his brothers, the brothers decided to get rid of Joseph. These two key decisions – by Jacob and by the brothers – had life-altering consequences. In today's family business, how you make decisions and deal with your frustrations may have similar long-term ramifications. Too often, family members don't think enough about the implications of their current path. If conflict is not managed, if concerns are not heard, if perceived unfair treatment is not addressed, bad things happen. (Bad things sometimes happen when these things are dealt with, but most assuredly happen if not attended to).

I once met with a potential client, a representative of a leading farm family in America. We spent a long session discussing many of the issues the family was facing. They needed help with compensation issues, help with informing heirs about what business assets they would likely inherit, help with family members reconciling after deep misunderstandings, help with siblings being able to talk about working together despite different management styles. When he finished, he asked what I would charge to help him. I asked him what it might be worth if some of those issues would be worked out positively – he got a big grin on his face and told me he couldn't pay me what is was worth – it was too valuable! This person realized the way that current decisions have important long-term consequences in the family business and family system.

These tough issues have important consequences that don't magically go away. You can't sweep them under the rug. At some point those issues will arise, and when they do you have a choice about how you deal with them.

Questions for Reflection and Discussion:

What have been some tough decisions made by your family business in the last few years? Have there been some difficult decisions you have avoided making?

What would have been the likely outcomes of the situation had you not made the decisions when you did?

Understanding these consequences, now turn to the future. What issues in your family business at this moment need to be dealt with? Differences in compensation? Past conflict? Succession plans? Family members coming back to the business? Estate plans? Make a list of crucial areas you need to address or decisions you need to make in your family business.

Chapter Four

When Temptation Comes
(Gen. 39:6-9)

"Now Joseph was handsome and good looking. And after a time his master's wife cast her eyes on Joseph and said, 'Lie with me.' But he refused and said to his master's wife, 'Look, with me here, my master has no concern about anything in the house, and he has put everything that he has in my hand. He is not greater in this house than I am, nor has he kept back anything from me except yourself, because you are his wife. How then could I do this great wickedness, and sin against God?'"

AT FIRST GLANCE, this text introduces us to a fairly straightforward story. Joseph, now in Egypt, is working for one of Pharaoh's key men. His employer's wife had amorous designs on him; Joseph refused her advances. In the next chapter we will see that he was punished for his fidelity to God and his employer. We readers then marvel at Joseph's steadfastness and are urged to be like him. End of story.

But on closer inspection, certain ambiguities or silences in the text either defy easy interpretation or leave us with lingering questions. We will get to these issues after following Joseph on his already tumultuous life journey.

We saw in our previous chapter that Joseph's brothers sold him to passing traders to get him out of their lives. The last words of Gen. 37 indicate that the traders actually were middlemen, and they in turn sold Joseph to a prominent household in Egypt. We leave Joseph there, and then in chapter 38 are introduced to another skeleton in the family closet—brother Judah ends up impregnating a daughter-in-law disguised as a prostitute. As those working with family businesses know, you really can't make this stuff up!

Then in this chapter, we return to Joseph in Egypt in the house of Potiphar, the captain of Pharaoh's guard. In a word, he experiences meteoric success. God is with him and his employer likes him too! Quick promotions follow, and the last words of v. 6 say it all, "he (Potiphar) had no concern for anything, but the food that he ate." Those last words mean that except for his food preparer, Joseph was the most trusted person in Potiphar's house.

Things Fall Apart

Two words (in Hebrew) change everything. Potiphar's wife says to Joseph, "Lie with me." The word translated "lie" is the common Hebrew word for lying down, such as when you lie down to sleep, though in Genesis it is mostly used for people "lying down" with those they shouldn't. The word is in the imperative voice, which means that it is in the form of a command, like a superior would give an inferior. So, Joseph faced a huge dilemma.

But is it strictly a temptation? We usually think of temptations as inducements to do something wrong that we are already a bit inclined to do, and we have no indication that Joseph had the slightest interest in Potiphar's wife. It would have been stupid of him to have this interest but we all know that when intimate relationships are involved, rational calculation often goes out the window. So, we don't know if this is really a temptation at all to Joseph, such as when a person says, "Gambling or drinking is no great temptation for me."

But if it was no temptation at all to Joseph, why did he stay around to try to explain himself? Was he trying to change her mind? To weigh the tensions between self-preservation and courtesy, both of which he wanted to honor? But look at his words. His first words are right on target—he refused her offer and then said that Potiphar has placed trust in him ("he has put everything he has in my hand") so that Potiphar has no worries in his house. This is a true and good statement, since it shows how Joseph understands what is at stake in his position. But a question arises....

Why Not Leave Immediately?

Joseph had probably said enough at this point. Yet he continued with these words: "He (Potiphar) is not greater in this house than I am, nor has he kept back anything from me except yourself, because you are his wife." Is Joseph's self-centeredness, which emerged earlier in the story and got him in trouble with his brothers in chapter 37, rearing its ugly head again? Why in this situation would he compare himself with his master and, basically, say that they were equal? What is the effect on Potiphar's wife, on us as readers, on Joseph as he says these words?

Then, Joseph goes on, addressing the wife and says that *you* alone are the only thing he has kept back from me. The Hebrew word for "keeping back," is a special one in Genesis, and it usually is coupled with an object of extreme value. Joseph keeps talking to her about how he has everything, except her. How might she hear this?

Joseph was no doubt in a no-win situation. And he may have contributed a slight bit to it. He had little time to decide on a strategy. He spoke. He fled. He left his garment behind. He suffered for it.

Reflection and Questions

✑ Reflection One: From Success to Excess then Distress

Personal or organizational success, whether in a family business or in other enterprises, might bring admiration, recognition, power, influence, wealth, options and opportunities. Many of those benefits can be used to influence others positively, but they can also be used to undermine progress, relationships, and even a legacy. The pages of national newspapers or business publications regularly detail the abuses and misdeeds of presidents and CEO's who took advantage of their power or financial access to benefit themselves to the detriment of their family, staff, partners or shareholders.

It appears that Potiphar's wife intended to use her power in just such a detrimental way. And it also appears that Joseph, while ultimately stepping away from the situation, again let his strengths inflate his ego and so he flirted with a disastrous situation. Just as earlier in our story, when he kept reminding his brothers that he was special, Joseph perhaps should have known when to quit talking, but he just couldn't help himself!

There are plenty of stories where unsatisfying marriages, attraction to co-workers, long hours together, and the "thrill of the new" destroy relationships in the family enterprise. But this passage is instructive beyond perceived or actual adultery. To those family business members with power, wealth and prestige – people who can often have about anything they want – temptation can come in many forms, that, when pursued to excess, can ultimately lead to a family business break-up. Here are a few more of the dangers I see often in family-owned businesses:

- Abusing substances (alcohol in particular)
- Purchasing unnecessary toys, from gadgets and guns to automobiles and airplanes
- An addiction to extravagant lifestyles – trips, houses, clothes and jewelry
- Hiding kickbacks or rebates or gifts from vendors from the company or other family members
- Avoiding taxes or not reporting income
- Misrepresenting time spent on company issues versus personal issues
- An addiction to work based on a singular focus on financial success
- Using company resources without fair compensation to the business

Questions for Reflection and Discussion:

Study the above list closely. Do you know any people in family businesses that have succumbed to these abuses or temptations? Are there some missing from the list?

Is your particular vulnerability on this list?

If you didn't keep your desires in check, how might your pursuit of those desires take away from the family business? How might it impact your family relationships?

✍ Reflection Two: The Importance of Trust

The deeper issue to consider here, beyond excesses, is the role of trust. What allows Potiphar's wife and Joseph to carry on their private conversation? Answer: they both held the trust of Potiphar. Potiphar's trust paved the way for interaction that blew up a seemingly great situation.

What happened here, in a word, was that the CEO's (Potiphar's) trust was broken. In a family business, trust is often a key element of the smooth functioning of the business. It almost goes without saying that family members should manage certain financial functions, key customer or landowner relationships, or the hiring of employees, because we trust and expect them to have the best interests of the family business at heart. I mean, if you can't trust your family members, whom can you trust?

But sometimes trust is hard to come by. Several years ago, during the initial phases of a project, I interviewed each member of an extended family. There were clear frustrations. The older brother had come back to the family business after "goofing around" and losing money in several post-college ventures, while the younger brother had not gone to college but had faithfully labored in the family business and had established significant wealth.

As the interviews progressed, I saw that the younger brother's children were wondering about the "commitment" of their cousins to the family business because their father had seemingly dropped his commitment for years. The older brother's children in turn wondered out loud whether the cousins were only in the business to milk it for their benefit. Was their commitment to shared family success or individual profit?

I saw then and there that unless I addressed the issue of trust in the family system, we could have little chance for success.

Questions for Reflection and Discussion:

Are you aware of situations where a breach of trust has occurred in a family business? What results followed from that breaking of trust?

If a family member violated your trust, could you continue in business together?

If trust begins to erode with one of your family business partners, are you willing to share your concerns with them?

Chapter Five

Ignored!

(Gen. 40:20-23)

"On the third day, which was Pharaoh's birthday, he made a feast for all his servants, and lifted up the head of the chief cupbearer and the head of the chief baker among his servants. He restored the chief cupbearer to his cupbearing, and he placed the cup in Pharaoh's hand; but the chief baker he hanged, just as Joseph had interpreted to them. Yet the chief cupbearer did not mention Joseph, but forgot him."

THIS CHAPTER DEALS with the difficult situation of how to handle rejection and neglect. The problem is made worse in this case because Joseph, an obviously talented person, was not just temporarily neglected; he was also forgotten. He languished in prison for years because of the encounter with Potiphar's wife, narrated in our previous chapter. In this chapter, we will explore the dynamics and feelings associated with that rejection.

Let's begin with the words of the last sentence of the Biblical passage just quoted. It says, "the chief cupbearer didn't mention Joseph, but forgot him." It would have been enough just to use the word "did not mention" but by using both verbs it is almost as if the author is trying to get us to stop and *think about* the experience of Joseph in prison. Not only was Joseph "not mentioned;" he was also "forgotten." There is a sort of helpless finality to the combination of these verbs. And, indeed, if we read on four more words, we see it is only "after two whole years…" (41:1) that something positive happens; i.e., it was a very costly forgetting for Joseph.

The one who "forgot" Joseph had been the recipient of Joseph's help. Just a few days previously, the chief cupbearer had a troubling dream, and since Joseph was skilled at dream interpretation, he was able to put an interpretation on the dream that actually was true and served to comfort the official. Joseph, as it were, was giving his "specialist" advice and his "fee" for such service was stated clearly by Joseph to the cupbearer, "But remember me when it is well with you," (40:14).

Not a chance. So overjoyed was the official at being restored that he just forgot Joseph. We aren't told why he forgot him. Perhaps the mention of Joseph to Pharaoh's officials might have complicated his own release. In any case, Joseph continued in prison another two years.

So, how did Joseph live in the reality of this rejection? Three points focus our discussion.

Keep Using Gifts To Serve

Joseph's being overlooked was the third in a series of mistreatments which he experienced. We have already seen the first two: being sold by his brothers and being imprisoned on false charges. And now, he is ignored at a crucial time. But what does he do? He keeps using his gifts to serve. In this case the gift emphasized was his skill at dream interpretation.

In antiquity the skill to interpret dreams was like being a combination of an economist, political scientist and a theologian.

Such a person could "read" the spiritual world as well as the realities of life before him. Such a person was very useful for emperors, because the control of these worlds was the basis of a ruler's power.

So, even though he had been mistreated and misjudged, he kept on working, using the skill with two of his fellow jailmates to remove the confusion from their minds about their dreams. But Joseph didn't mince words; he didn't always give pleasant interpretations. In one case he predicted that the chief baker would be hanged—which he was. But ultimately it was this skill that came to Pharaoh's attention when he had a troubling dream that defied interpretation (41:1-8). The cupbearer finally remembered Joseph, and Joseph used his gifts to interpret Pharaoh's dilemma and get out of prison.

Interpret Life as Under God's Care

A key to Joseph's being able to serve well was his ability to see the meaning of his life not simply from the perspective of his immediate injustice but from the perspective of God's care. This point will especially come out in our final chapter, but is already hinted at here. Joseph suffers human injustice but, in whatever situation that results, God is with him. Joseph most clearly adopts this perspective when he says to his compatriots in prison, trying to encourage them to confide in him, "Do not interpretations (of dreams) belong to God? Please tell them to me" (40:8).

Confidence in One's Abilities

Note the combination of humility and confidence in this just-quoted statement. On the one hand is the recognition that God alone has the key to this special area of life—dream interpretation. But, at the same time Joseph is confident that if God knows it, then Joseph knows it! So, then, speak it out, and I, Joseph, will give you the true interpretation of it!

One of the first casualties of suffering injustice is the feeling that we have either misjudged our abilities, that the world is stacked against us, or that things are irretrievably lost to us. It is not as if Joseph was languishing in prison for the triumph of an idea. He was suffering, instead, because of someone's personal pique. Yet Joseph seemed to retain a kind of quiet confidence in his abilities, a feeling that he still was valuable even if not in the "center" of things, and he kept on working...

Reflection and Questions

✥ Reflection One: Forgotten in the Family Business

Family members participating in a business together are enmeshed in three systems, which I alternatively describe as wearing three hats: a *family member* hat, a *management* or employee hat, and a hat as a current *owner* or potential heir.

Taking these in reverse order, the owner or potential heir invokes the language of a shareholder: What are my assets worth, and what is my return on my investment? The employee or manager uses the lens of meritocracy: Am I recognized (paid) for my role and the contribution I make to the success of the organization? But when focused on the family system, the currency is often love, governed by a principle of equality: Do I feel loved and how do I show my love to others? With all three perspectives (love, merit, economic value) usually operating at once, it's no wonder that conflict and confusion are hallmarks of family business!

It is also not unusual for a family member to feel forgotten – just as Joseph felt – in one of those systems. For one family business member I know, a main source of pain for him is that he has made a strong effort in the family system to repair relationships, but feels that he has received no acknowledgement for his effort. He knows the effort he has expended—to contact people, hear them out, reassure them of their value, encourage them to support each other—but he would just like to be recognized for his efforts every once in a while.

This person feels forgotten, and even taken for granted, as he thinks no one has seen his efforts. After working with the family, I know that his efforts have not gone unnoticed, and I've encouraged him to continue to do this, as he may uniquely be positioned to be the family reconciler. But, learning how to deal with his feeling is key to effective participation in the family business system.

Questions for Reflection and Discussion:

Have you ever felt that your contributions have gone unrecognized in the family business?

What was the situation?

Do you find it difficult to continue making contributions, even if they go unnoticed?

❦ Reflection Two: The Family Business as Prison

Joseph's being trapped in prison is an interesting metaphor for those who think about family businesses. While most of the time we talk about all of the positive aspects of closely held companies, sometimes the family company can seem more like a trap, or even a prison cell.

This was the experience of one member of a family, call him Jim, I worked with several years ago. Jim felt trapped because the family business was really not his first choice. During college he pursued subjects not related to business, but he later struggled to find a career and ended up back at home, in the family enterprise. He had been in the business for a decade but clearly wished he were elsewhere.

As I was meeting with the family and discussing each family member's hopes, goals and strengths, Jim suddenly stood up, asked for a few minutes to address the group, and proceeded to announce that he was leaving the business. All were surprised by the suddenness and seeming finality of his words.

After the shock of his announcement wore off, and people thought about his strengths and the role he had been playing in the organization, they understood his decision and actually rallied around him in his choice. They supported him emotionally and financially as he explored new options. Had they not had the meeting, he likely would have continued to be unhappy in his role, and others would have been unhappy interacting with him as well. Thus the key to his leaving the "prison" of family business was a recognition of his strengths, passion and interest, and the support of the family to pursue those, regardless of whether they were exercised inside or outside of the family enterprise.

Questions for Reflection and Discussion:

What are some situations where people feel trapped, or imprisoned, in life?

Spouses who had their own careers and then "followed" their partner to the family business often feel as if they have lost their identity. This happens not just with family members but also with key employees. Has this happened in your organization?

How do people get into feelings of entrapment? Why don't people speak up sooner when they are sinking into this isolation or confinement?

Do you think that any members of your family/family business (you included) feel this sense of isolation, entrapment or imprisonment today in their life or work?

Chapter Six

The Conflict Deepens
(Gen. 42:14-17)

"But Joseph said to them, 'It is just as I have said to you; you are spies! Here is how you shall be tested: as Pharaoh lives, you shall not leave this place unless your youngest brother comes here! Let one of you go and bring your brother, while the rest of you remain in prison, in order that your words may be tested, whether there is truth in you; or else, as Pharaoh lives, surely you are spies.' And he put them all together in prison for three days."

THIS CHAPTER PRESENTS the next episode in our complex family drama. Here we will do two things: return to one aspect of Genesis 37 that led to the sibling confrontation of this passage; and think about the way the brothers talk in the passage just cited. We will explore two significant issues in family relationships: improper assumptions and miscommunication. Both are front and center as the conflict deepens.

False Assumptions (Further Thoughts on Genesis 37)

There is one lingering issue from Genesis 37 that invites

mention. You recall from our discussion that the brothers, incensed at Joseph's narcissistic dreaming, decided to sell him to passing traders to be rid of him. This, actually, was the more "merciful" route, as some of the brothers had argued for killing Joseph outright. But they got rid of their brother cleanly, so they thought, by selling him to the tradesmen. The price is never mentioned. Middle Eastern culture places a lot of emphasis on haggling over price; you wonder if the brothers did this before selling Joseph.

Well, at least they were rid of him. But they had to be able to tell their father something convincing about their brother's disappearance. So they concocted a scheme rich in symbolism to deceive their father. They took the colorful robe, the object both of the father's favoritism and the brothers' hatred, dipped it in blood, and showed it to the father *without explanation*. I italicize those words because it was a deliberate part of the brothers' strategy. They let the father draw an immediate conclusion so that they wouldn't have to lie actively.

So, the father assumed the worst. In fact, the text of Genesis 37 spends several verses describing Jacob's grief. His emotion is captured in these words: "he refused to be comforted and said, 'No, I shall go down to Sheol to my son, mourning" (37:35). The language used is that of finality; the beloved son is gone, the father is inconsolable, nothing will change.

All this emerges from an assumption drawn from a lie. Do we draw a distinction between an actual lie, where you baldly say to someone something that is false, or a "passive" lie, where you let a person draw an erroneous conclusion and don't intervene to correct that conclusion? Are they morally equivalent? We are never told, but what we do see is how the lie corrodes family life. It has destroyed the father Jacob; it will also make him overprotective towards his other son through Rachel (Benjamin); it will make the brothers end up doing unhealthy things (Genesis 38 details one of those things). A lie and the assumptions drawn from it have driven a wedge in the family dynamics of the chosen clan.

Miscommunication (42:14-17)

In the midst of this development, need forces their collective hand. In this case the call, or the need, is food. Famine in Israel forced Jacob to send his sons to Egypt to buy grain. In order to forestall repetition of the earlier disaster, Jacob kept his youngest son through Rachel, Benjamin, close by his side at home. You sometimes wonder what it was like growing up as Benjamin after Joseph's disappearance, though we are never brought into Benjamin's psyche.

So, the 10 brothers go to Egypt to buy grain. The verses quoted above show that their encounter with the Egyptian official is none other than a meeting with their brother Joseph. But Joseph is unrecognizable to them because of his garments and changed features, and the effect of the meeting is like looking through a one-way mirror, where one party "sees" the other, but the other party is "blind." The 10 brothers want to buy grain, but Joseph will have other designs.

You wonder for a moment whether the money they will use to buy grain is that which they "earned" from selling their brother to the traders. In any case, Joseph stops them dead in their tracks by talking family, rather than talking grain. He addresses the brothers at the family's most vulnerable point—the safety of little Benjamin, and he refuses to transact business with brothers unless they bring Benjamin down to Egypt. Of course, this would expose the beloved son to abuse and possible death, but Joseph now is completely exploiting the vulnerability of his brothers. It is a naked power play. Perhaps he is saying to them, "See what it feels like! Don't you know I felt like this when you guys were deciding whether to kill me or not!?"

Reflection and Questions

✍ Reflection One: Assumptions and How They Damage

If I had a dollar for every time during a family meeting I heard a family member say "I just assumed you wanted…." I would be wealthy beyond imagination! Just as Jacob assumed the worst about Joseph based on the story the brothers told – or in this case, *didn't* tell – assumptions in today's family business can cause long-lasting pain.

I often work with fathers and sons who don't communicate well with each other. In one instance, the son seemed unhappy, and the father assumed it was because the son regretted his decision to return to the farm based on some comments he heard his son make about his friends' chosen careers. Meanwhile, the son never really heard his dad express appreciation for his returning to the farm after college, so he wasn't sure dad really wanted him there. In both cases, the assumptions each party was making, interspersed with some occasional conflict, led the son to quit farming and to move away. But in this case, neither party wanted, or was happy with, the outcome that came to pass. They let their assumptions determine their course of action, and they both came to regret it.

Many assumptions in the family business happen because there is a lack of communication about events or plans. I often say that in the absence of a good story, people make one up. In other words, without good communication people make assumptions about other's reasons, intentions and goals. And those assumptions can often result in just as much damage as an outright lie.

Questions for Reflection and Discussion:

Have you ever been the victim of someone's assumptions?

Did someone – did you – ever choose a course of action because of what you *thought* a person might or might not want, only to be mistaken?

As you consider your family business partners and the future of the organization, what assumptions might you be making about other people – their plans, their roles or their goals?

✑ Reflection Two: Talking Past Each Other

The brothers, having no way of knowing who Joseph really is, want to talk strictly in economic terms: How can they buy some grain? But Joseph wants to talk about the family: Bring me Benjamin! So it goes in family business. Sometimes some of the people are talking business, while other people are talking family. The result is additional confusion and misunderstanding.

An example of this kind of multi-level conversation occurred in family in which the daughter returned to the business. At work she would call her father by his first name. Over time, this practice came to bother, perhaps even hurt, her father. After all, she was his "little princess" and he could not see a reason why she wouldn't call him "Daddy." Was she trying to distance herself from her father?

During a facilitated discussion, the daughter shared that she was calling her dad by his first name so that other managers and employees in the business wouldn't think she was asking for, or getting, special treatment as a family member. By establishing herself through communication as a "normal" employee, she hoped to mitigate the appearance of favoritism. She was approaching the situation from an employee-management standpoint. Dad on the other hand, could only see himself in a father-family position. But once he heard and understood his daughter's desire to be seen as a normally-treated employee, he got it. They needed to speak the same language. Competency was driving her communication, love was driving his.

If we return to Joseph, then, we can see that the brothers are talking with an economic or business perspective, but Joseph is totally focused on the family. There can be no forward movement until both parties are in the same ballpark with their language.

Questions for Reflection and Discussion:

Have you ever had conversations about family business matters which just don't connect with the other person because you and he/she are talking on two different levels?

As you think about your family business conversations, how might you better clarify which "hat" you are wearing when talking to your family members?

When you are speaking to your siblings or parents or adult offspring, is it clear when you do so as their boss (the management system), their partners (the ownership system), or their family members (the family system)?

Chapter Seven

Desperation All Around
(Gen 42:36-38)

"And their father Jacob said to them, 'I am the one you have bereaved of children: Joseph is no more, and Simeon is no more, and now you would take Benjamin. All this has happened to me!' Then Reuben said to his father, 'You may kill my two sons if I do not bring him back to you. Put him in my hands, and I will bring him back to you.' But he said, 'My son shall not go down with you, for his brother is dead, and he alone is left. If harm should come to him on the journey that you are to make, you would bring down my gray hairs with sorrow to Sheol.' "

THIS EPISODE HAPPENS almost right on the heels of our preceding chapter. The brothers returned to their father with the news that they left Simeon with the strange man in Egypt and that they also must bring Benjamin to Egypt in order to secure Simeon's release. The news that Jacob must send Benjamin, his youngest son, to Egypt, sends him over the edge, and the conversation just quoted brings us into the heart of that desperation. As we examine it, we will see expressions of grief, hopelessness, self-pity, finality and, perhaps not unexpectedly, continuing family denial.

A Bundle of Emotions

As just mentioned, the demand of Joseph that the brothers bring Benjamin down to Egypt in order to free Simeon sends the family into convulsions of grief. In this passage only Jacob and Reuben, the oldest, speak. Jacob first expresses his despair in staccato-like language. The Hebrew only needs two words to express the first two thoughts: 'Joseph gone; Simeon gone!' Then, there are two three-word phrases: 'You take Benjamin; onme (one word in Hebrew) all this.' It is all so matter-of-fact, as if the final chapter of the family's life has already been written. And, the placement of the Hebrew words in the last phrase is interesting. The personal pronoun "on me" is placed first. It is as if Jacob is saying, 'look at me, I am the innocent party, and all this has just come upon me!' In the moment where some clear-headed thinking is needed, all Jacob can do is sink into his private pity party.

Reuben's response, if anything, makes things worse. His desperation matches his father's self-pity. As if to comfort his father, he offers up the life of his two sons if he doesn't return from Egypt with Benjamin safely in tow. It is almost like the line that we sometimes hear in desperate family situations, "If I kill myself, would that make you feel better?"

But Reuben is worse than that, because he offers up not his own life but the lives of *his two sons*. His convoluted logic seems to be, "if you lose Benjamin, and I then lose my two sons, we will be equal in a way, and that ought to mitigate your grief." Unreality has now completely overcome the family. Jacob has jumped to an unhelpful (and incorrect) conclusion and Reuben joins him by offering to cut off his posterity for the sake of the family.

Jacob's final words are almost anticlimactic. He seems

resolutely to decide not to send Benjamin (a decision that will soon be reversed), and then he bemoans his future fate if his sons aren't returned intact. He will, as he says, go down to Sheol with sorrow. Newsflash to Jacob: you are already there.

Reflection and Questions

✍ Reflection One: From "Poor, Poor Me" to "Possibility"

No one could doubt that Jacob has it bad. This episode with Benjamin leads him to focus on all the things that are going the way he doesn't want them to go, on all the things that are out of control in his life – even though later on, when Benjamin and Joseph connect, their reunion is key to the family's path to reconciliation. Jacob has mistaken the bleak present for the ultimate future.

One lesson, then, is to leave open the possibility that the situation you find yourself in might be used for a greater good. Or, alternatively, that the situation you are in now is not the final word in life. Of course it is hard to see such opportunities in the midst of difficulty, but simply asking the question "How can this situation be used for good?" might mean the difference between a life of bitterness and anger, and a life of positive influence on those around you.

Over the years I've worked with several families where massive conflict led to dramatic dissolution. Some families decided to split up their business; some individual members of the families, before the split, chose to exit the business. The difficulty of working together became too stressful and painful, prompting what some would consider a tragedy – the dissolution of the family business and its assets. And during the process of splitting, feelings were quite negative: something that at one time had seemed so promising was now ending so painfully.

Yet in several cases, in the ensuing years after the split, the family relationships got better. What had seemed to be a major disappointment had actually created opportunities for a different kind of interaction. People once constrained by the assumptions of family in a business setting were now free to blossom elsewhere. A new and different family narrative was created. In short, the situation became better but it took some processing of a difficult, tragic situation to make it so.

For example, one family I worked with did a poor job of including in-laws in discussions about the family business. The in-laws heard everything second-hand, through the filter of their spouses, which sometimes did not correctly reflect the parents' intentions. As the assumptions of unfairness mounted – each in-law thought their spouse was contributing more to the business and family success than the others (and their perception was reinforced by relentless comparisons among and between the siblings in the business) – the tension at family gatherings, business or otherwise, grew untenable. Eventually two of the family members asked to have their portion of the business "carved out" so they could go on their own, and we split the company.

In the discussions leading up to the split, people were very upset. The parents felt like their life's work was being torn apart, and the adult children and their spouses felt like they had given up promising financial, career and location opportunities elsewhere to devote themselves to a failed venture. Yet as the years progressed and each family member developed their own business or career, they came to see that the split had provided unique opportunities to create a new family and business narrative. And they eventually came to family events with considerably less stress than the years in which they were in business together. It took some time, but the situation that at one point looked so bleak eventually led to healthier family relationships.

Questions for Reflection and Discussion:

Whom do you know who is, like Jacob, angry, bitter or resentful because of something tragic or unexpectedly painful that happened in their life?

Do you know anyone who has overcome their tragedy and now offers a positive example of using a difficult situation for good?

What difference do those approaches make to the others around them – family members, employees, and neighbors?

ꮺ Reflection Two: A Race to the Unreasonable

Jacob and Reuben get into an interesting conversation that quickly reaches into the realm of the unreasonable, even the surreal, involving more family members in a terribly negative scenario. This also occurs occasionally in today's family businesses. For example, take the process of succession, which requires the senior generation to let go and the junior generation to step up and grab the reins. From years of facilitating such discussions, I know that this handoff is one of the most frustrating family business experiences many operations will go through. It offers a window into the role of emotions in the family business.

At the height of exasperation, each party becomes a little unreasonable: the parents seem reluctant to part with their hard-won success, and so the sons and daughters start talking about quitting, or starting their own business. The problem is that these businesses are usually capital intensive and splitting them is not an efficient use of the family's financial or human resources. The parents, in response, start talking about "just walking away", as if they have no emotional stake in something that five minutes previously they were hesitant to part with. The children then don't take the parents seriously and accuse them of denial and avoidance.

All of this serves to eliminate the opportunity to transfer the senior generation's considerable perspective and wisdom gathered over a generation or more. Neither the act of simply walking away nor a tightfisted holding on makes good business sense, but emotions drive the interaction. Before you know it, people are planning or executing an exit that not only decreases the chance of future success, but also runs the risk of further damaging family relationships.

Questions for Reflection and Discussion:

Do you know of a situation in your family or family business where reason went right out the window, and only competing, irreconcilable emotions were left?

What is the most frustrating experience you have right now in your family business?

If you could "step to the balcony" (a phrase we use in conflict resolution when trying to get parties to see their current situation), what are some reasonable solutions to the problems faced by the organization?

Chapter Eight

On the Precarious Edge
(Gen. 43:26-30)

"When Joseph came home, they brought him the presents that they had carried into the house, and bowed to the ground before him. He inquired about their welfare, and said, 'Is your father well, the old man of whom you spoke? Is he still alive?' They said, 'Your servant our father is well; he is still alive.' And they bowed their heads and did obeisance. Then he looked up and saw his brother Benjamin, his mother's son, and said, 'Is this your youngest brother, of whom you spoke to me? God be gracious to you, my son!' With that, Joseph hurried out, because he was overcome with affection for his brother, and he was about to weep. So he went into a private room and wept there."

THIS PASSAGE EXPLORES deep emotions that cannot be expressed. The emotions arise from a complex network of interlocking family relationships, and in this passage these emotions threaten to unravel the entire family dynamic. Everyone is trapped in his own private drama, and the oppressiveness of these dramas keeps people from talking to one another. This passage encourages us to ask the question of what things *cannot be spoken* in our family dynamics, and how those things that cannot be spoken may threaten to undo us.

The Competing Dramas of Genesis 43

Three dramas unfold before us in this passage. On the surface, most obviously, is Joseph's drama. He is looking through the "one way" mirror towards his brothers, recognizing them without himself being recognized. He was betrayed and mistreated by 10 of them, but he has a soft spot in his heart for the 11th, his younger brother Benjamin. Benjamin was too young to collude with the older brothers in selling Joseph and is likewise a son of Jacob through Rachel. Joseph's heart longs for Benjamin, but he can't express this longing or else he will reveal his identity. If he reveals his identity, he cannot continue to toy with the emotions and vulnerability of the older brothers. Thus, Joseph *wants* to speak and help resolve the family dilemma, but he cannot. He is trapped between his need for connection and need for revenge on the 10 brothers.

Then, there is what I call the "10 brothers drama." They had sold Joseph into captivity, they had then come down to Egypt to buy grain and were forced to leave one of their number, Simeon, as hostage with Joseph so that they would, in fact, return with their brother Benjamin. Disagreements flared up among the brothers as they settled upon a strategy. Indeed, I would do anything to have heard the discussion leading to the decision to leave Simeon alone in Egypt as hostage until they later returned with Benjamin in tow.

The 10 brothers drama is heightened because of their continuing vulnerability to Joseph. Grain supplies run out again and they must return, with all kinds of gifts in tow to "buy"

Joseph's good will. But they return also with Benjamin, the most precious cargo of all. They know that this strange Egyptian person whom they met (who happens to be their brother Joseph) could easily take Benjamin and imprison or kill him, an act that would send the father Jacob into incalculable and irreversible pain. They cannot voice their fears, for to whom would they speak them? If Joseph is trapped by his emotions, they are trapped by their circumstances.

Then there is the drama of the father, Jacob. When he first sent the brothers to Egypt to buy grain, he kept Benjamin home, reasoning that if he lost his youngest son, along with Joseph, his life would be less than worthless. At least by keeping Benjamin with him he could try to salvage a smidgen of security. But now he has to relinquish Benjamin to fulfill Joseph's demand. No doubt he had thought in his mind that he would rather sacrifice the hostage, Simeon, and keep his son Benjamin close by his side. But now that possibility is taken away from him. Benjamin must go to Egypt now, because the family is in want and there is nowhere else to turn.

Conclusion

So, each of the three is imprisoned in his own unspeakable drama—Joseph by emotion, the 10 brothers by circumstances, and Jacob by grief. The collective weight of these three dramas is that no one can *speak* what needs to be said. No one is free, even though all the tools to address their problem and potentially solve it are right before them. Their relationships, rather than empowering them, immobilize them. The family is on the precarious edge. It really could go either way…

Reflection and Questions

✎ Reflection: Caught in the Middle

The three dramas mentioned here are rich: emotion, conflict, strategy and suspense contribute to a fascinating look at a family situation from multiple perspectives. The commonality is that no one can outwardly speak of the way they are feeling or how others are acting; family members are "caught" between the emotions of their different options. Joseph is caught between wanting relationship and wanting revenge. The brothers are caught between the revelation of their fears and realization of their survival. Jacob is caught between the sacrifice of Benjamin and security of his broader family. To communicate out-loud the feelings around each option would create vulnerability, harm egos, expose intentions, damage relationships or demonstrate weakness.

And guess what? Those are the same fears that limit families today from tackling the drama in their organizational relationships. This feeling of being caught, of not being able to express what your true feelings are, leads people to not speak at all, to bottle-up their emotions and ideas. Figuratively speaking it's as if the tension between two poles has tightened the lips and mouth of each family member, rendering them unable to say the things that might in fact help the situation.

The feeling of being caught is at the root of many family business struggles. Take the case of a newly married family member who has just returned to the business and is working long hours to establish his commitment and credibility to other family members in the business. He often feels caught between wanting to spend time with his new spouse and wanting to prove himself to the family. If he expresses this feeling to his family, his parents, brothers or sisters may question his commitment. If he opens up to his spouse, it may signal conflict at a very early stage in the marriage.

Either option feels like a no-win situation. So, he remains silent.

Another example of feeling caught surfaces with parents who had some children return to the business and others who did not. They love their children, but feel that some have perhaps invested more in creating or preserving the family's wealth than others. If they openly express their appreciation for those that returned, they might alienate those that didn't return (and further reduce the chance that they might return someday). Yet if the parents don't express their appreciation, the kids that did return don't feel acknowledged for the contributions they've made. Again, the feeling of being caught is pervasive, and the easier, short-term answer is to not say anything.

In transitions of leadership, power and decision-making in a family business, there is a point where the senior generation feels caught between their own feelings of mortality and usefulness, and desire to hand the baton to the next generation. Mom and Dad wonder that if they hand over the reins, they may be put out to pasture…yet they feel they can still provide some help, wisdom and guidance. Meanwhile, the younger generation feels caught between their desire for more autonomy and the respect they feel they should show to their parents. They wonder that if they begin to exercise too much leadership, will they somehow be communicating that their parents are not valued in the business? Both generations' feelings can lead to a deafening silence on the issue of management succession – the timing, expectations and responsibilities in the handing of power from one generation to the next – thus decreasing the already difficult odds of a successful transition.

As you can see, feeling caught lends itself to many situations in the family business. The way out requires communicating – opening up – about feelings, concerns or desires. The risk, of course, is that you hurt someone, including yourself, with your words. More often than not, however, staying silent incurs an even greater risk.

Questions for Reflection and Discussion:

Have you ever found it difficult to express your true feelings to your family members? What was the occasion? Have you had a negative experience when doing so in the past?

What are some of the more difficult issues your family business faces? Do you feel "caught" between options? Do you think others feel caught as well?

What are the pros and cons of discussing each person's feelings on the most important issues in your family business?

Chapter Nine

Found Out!

(Gen. 44:16-17)

"And Judah said, 'What can we say to my lord? What can we speak? How can we clear ourselves? God has found out the guilt of your servants; here we are then, my lord's slaves, both we and also the one in whose possession the cup has been found.' But he (Joseph) said, 'Far be it from me that I should do so! Only the one in whose possession the cup was found shall be my slave; but as for you, go up in peace to your father.'"

LIFE CONTINUES. The brothers bought grain from Joseph and began the return journey to their father, and this time all eleven brothers were finally together. It seems as if, contrary to expectations, things are going to work out after all! I could imagine the anticipation of the brothers as they left Joseph, just waiting to clear the Egyptian border so that they would be safely at home in Israel.

But they didn't know that Joseph had undermined them further, by planting his favorite silver cup in Benjamin's sack. Thus, when Joseph sent out a party to overtake the brothers, accusing them of stealing from him, Joseph was setting the brothers up for their final humiliation. They swore that none of them had stolen anything of Joseph's. So sure were they of this that they solemnly pledged that anyone who had the silver cup would be subject to the death penalty at Joseph's hand. Of course, as the story unfolds, the silver cup was found in Benjamin's sack. Thus they admitted the most damning line of all—helpless little brother Benjamin, the one they had vowed to protect, should get the death penalty. At that moment, the brothers felt as vulnerable, helpless, and desperate as their father Jacob. Everything, it seemed, had irretrievably collapsed—again.

Once Again, The Brothers Talk

This time, when the brothers appear before Joseph, it is Judah and Joseph who speak. The brothers' desperation is palpable. But even in this vulnerable position, Judah tries to "negotiate." First, he recognizes their guilt before God. But then, he subtly changes the terms of the earlier statement. Rather than having Benjamin facing the death penalty alone, Judah proposes, quite matter-of-factly, that *all* the brothers should now be Joseph's *servants*. This would at least "help" the brothers in two ways: they might be able to keep their eyes on little Benjamin, and they wouldn't have to return home to face the impossible combination of their father's grief, rage and despair.

But Joseph didn't get to his high station in Egyptian life without skills. He sees through Judah's proposal and slices him verbally to bits. But he does so with the kind of false courtesy and false magnanimity that actually will bring the whole family drama to a head.

Listen to Joseph's first words, "Far be it from me that I should do so!" That is, 'I couldn't think of having *all 11* of you as servants as you propose. That would be unjust of me, Joseph.' Then, he goes on with the most chilling part of his decision. He says, as it were, 'Leave the little guy. I won't even execute him, but I will simply make him my slave.'

Then, as if to rub their faces in their vulnerability even more, he says, 'The ten of you, well, you simply can run along home in peace to your dad.' What??? Go *in peace* back to Jacob? Joseph certainly knows the family dynamics, even if they weren't fully told him by his brothers. Sending the brothers back to Jacob with grain but no Benjamin would absolutely break the father's heart. No question about it. But to add the sting, "go up in *peace*" to your father, well, that is piling insult on injury.

The brothers are now Joseph's playthings, and they know it. They are now as vulnerable to Joseph as Joseph was to the brothers when they were debating whether to kill him or sell him to passing traders. The shoe is completely on the other foot. Taste it, bros!

Reflection and Questions

✒ Reflection: Relationship Imbalance, Equalizing Pain, and Conflict "Ripeness"

During a seminar in college, Jim Wallis, the long-time editor of *Sojourners* magazine, talked about defining "justice" as a process of restoring right relationships. In other words, achieving justice meant bringing people at odds back into positive alignment with one another.

In some ways, this part of Joseph's story is his chance to set the stage for justice, for a positive alignment of relationships. What could he have done? For one thing, when the brothers were brought back to him in their vulnerable state, Joseph could simply have said, 'I am Joseph. I planted this silver chalice in the little one's bag in order to trap you and make you feel vulnerable. But now that I have accomplished that goal, I am ready to bury the hatchet, to restore relationships.' In the words of Jim Wallis, he could have done what he could to bring "positive alignment" back to the family. But he doesn't do so at this point. Why not?

I think at this point in the story we see evidence of a profound but often-overlooked phenomenon, the need to "balance" the pain in both parties before true reconciliation can happen. That is, if we try to rush too quickly to cover over the hurt, to try to proclaim a relationship breach healed before both sides truly feel ready to admit their vulnerability, pain and readiness for reconciliation, we could short-circuit the process of reconciliation and, in fact, derail the entire effort. In a word, sometimes conflict isn't yet "ripe" for resolution.

When Conflict Isn't Yet "Ripe" for Resolution

So, instead of pushing for reconciliation at this point, Joseph increases the brothers' anxiety. By planning to keep Benjamin with him and send the rest of the brothers home, Joseph would be creating a deeper sense of despair in the brothers that might have matched his own hopelessness when abandoned to the slave traders so many years ago. Both sides may now begin to have a common experience of loss and grief whereas prior to Joseph's toying with his brothers, they could have no understanding of how deep Joseph's pain might have been.

The type of relationship imbalance where one party is more deeply offended than the other often fuels family business conflict. At some point in the history of family business interaction, whether it is between siblings, cousins, in-laws, or generations, someone has been hurt. The pain may have been intentionally inflicted, like in this case between Joseph and his brothers. Or, the pain may arise from actions that were unintended to cause pain. In either case, people feel the pain and then begin responding to the pain.

For example, I've seen great pain created because a mother acknowledged one daughter-in-law's needs but not another's because she felt the first daughter-in-law was in need of attention. Or, a gift was given to a grandson but the same gift was not given to another due to misunderstood communication with the grandson's parents. In another case, one sibling had the chance to return to the business but others did not, but not all siblings understood that the business couldn't afford to have them all come back. In all of these situations, the offended or slighted party first reacted to pain in a way that furthered family conflict.

Let me offer another, a more typical example. In a family business, one brother (insert "other family member") who is loud, aggressive, and sees every situation as a win-lose negotiation often "runs over" a brother who is soft-spoken, introverted, and focused on the quality of relationships. The first brother does not necessarily intend to do things that hurt his brother, but that is what happens due to the way he approaches situations and how he is "wired."

To feel some sense of justice, then, the second brother (or other family member) usually intentionally looks for ways to make his brother feel some semblance of pain. The first brother, unaware of the impact of his behaviors, cannot understand why his brother would purposefully want to hurt him. And, it's not that the offended party necessarily wants to hurt the offender, but they know of no other way to restore a sense of balance to the relationship.

Conflicts escalate because people are often reaching for ways to respond to hurt. They get caught in a cycle of responding to the pain someone else has caused them, and before you know it we're in a cyclone of negative interaction. If Joseph's brothers had any leverage at this point in the story, I can imagine they might have tried to use it and we could have seen more conflict. But Joseph's domination of the situation was complete.

In this case the conflict between Joseph and his brothers continued because it was not yet "ripe" for resolution. By being attentive to the question, "Is it now time to try to resolve the conflict?" you can bring enormous wisdom and insight into difficult family dynamics.

Questions for Reflection and Discussion:

When have you been hurt by a family member? Were they aware of the pain they caused you?

Have you ever tried to solve a problem or resolve a conflict before it was "ready" or "ripe" to be solved?

What are some examples you have seen, or can imagine, where one family member perpetuated the cycle of conflict in the family and perhaps created an untenable family/family business situation?

Chapter Ten

Reconciliation At Last!

(Gen. 45:1-4, 14)

"Then Joseph could no longer control himself before all those who stood by him, and he cried out, 'Send everyone away from me.' So no one stayed with him when Joseph made himself known to his brothers. And he wept so loudly that the Egyptians heard it, and the household of Pharaoh heard it. Joseph said to his brothers, 'I am Joseph. Is my father still alive?' But his brothers could not answer him, so dismayed were they at his presence.... And he kissed all his brothers and wept upon them; and after that his brothers talked with him."

RECONCILIATION HAPPENS. SOMETIMES. In this chapter we will explore two keys to reconciliation that emerge from this story, a story that is among the most dramatic and poignant family scenes in the Scriptures. The two keys presented here are a willingness to reveal oneself honestly and a demonstration of genuine affection. But before we get to this "payoff," we have to follow the brothers through one more peril.

The Dynamics of Reconciliation

As we saw in our previous chapter, the brothers returned to Joseph and threw themselves at his feet begging for mercy, fully aware that now they were paying the price for their own maltreatment of Joseph. Judah's desperate speech at the end of Genesis 44 (18-34) is remarkable in several ways, perhaps the most notable of which is that in these verses the word "father" is mentioned no less than 15 times! The passage is like a great ocean wave coming towards shore, with every mention of "father" acting as another wave pounding in a rising crescendo on the beach. The word "father" rings in Joseph's ears like an unending chorus, and it may have been this repeated use of "father" that convinces Joseph that the issue really is not just between him and his brothers or his desire for revenge, but is about the future of the family. If Joseph acts responsibly now, he can save the family.

Gen. 45 opens. It is a passage layered with emotional richness. Joseph makes the first move. After sending everyone out of the room except the brothers, the Scriptures just say, "So no one stayed with him when Joseph made himself known to his brothers" (v. 2). His words were simple, direct, to the point. "I am Joseph. Is my father still alive?"

The first key to reconciliation is the willingness to reveal yourself, honestly, to the people whom you have hurt and have hurt you. When he says, "I am Joseph," he is not only reframing the entire relationship, but he is as much as saying 'I am ready to reveal myself to you, to tell you my side of the story, to let you in on the truth as I see it.' But he does more. Those few following words, "Is my father still alive," are significant because he shows through these that he wants to be *reintegrated* into the family. He not only wants to tell his own truth, but he wants to do so in the context of a restored relationship with his father.

But there is even more on this first point. When he reveals himself to his brothers, their first reaction *wasn't* gratitude. The Hebrew word used to describe the brothers' reaction in verse 4 can be translated "to be terrified, agitated, amazed, confounded." That is, their first reaction was a combination of fear and amazement. Perhaps, they thought, this strange man was just setting them up again!

The final verse gives us the second key to reconciliation—reconciliation really doesn't take place until genuine affection is demonstrated. Until Joseph and the brothers actually *touched* each other, suspicions could remain. Even the tears might be manufactured. But the tears and hugs, the kisses and sighs, showed that the desire to reveal the truth of the matter was genuine. Here we have both genuine truth *and* genuine affection.

At its most basic, reconciliation is both a *strange* and *wonderful* thing. It is strange because it moves the relationship in a different direction, one that really wasn't expected at all. It is wonderful because it eventually leads to the question, "Is my father still alive?"—i.e., how can we call get back together? Reconciliation was *strange* to the Egyptians, because they wondered why Joseph was crying. He wasn't acting in "character." It was strange, at first, to the brothers. But the stronger word is that it was *wonderful*. Honesty and genuine affection would triumph over the corrosive effects of alienation, subterfuge and guilt.

Reflection and Questions

✎ Reflection One: A Most Difficult Undertaking

Many family businesses experience conflict; few experience reconciliation. Why? Because it is *hard*. To reveal yourself honestly to someone who has hurt you involves dredging up the emotions linked to the origins of the conflict. The anger, the pain, the frustration…you've worked through all of those feelings, and to spend time honestly communicating with the person(s) who hurt you brings back the trauma of the conflict. Joseph "wept so loudly…that the household of Pharaoh heard it." I can imagine all the feelings of being abandoned as a youth by one's family were coming back to the surface. Who wants to go through that again?

Reconciliation is also *risky*. What if you are ready to reveal yourself to the other person, but they are not ready to hear it? What if your willingness to truly reconcile is not matched by the other party's desire to reconnect? Will the emotional effort and pain involved in preparing for reconciliation be wasted? Just like one takes a chance when loving someone for the first time, reconciliation involves a risk of pain – again – with someone who has already hurt you once. Sometimes the pain and the risk, and the fact that family members have grown comfortable with emotional distance, leads people to decide that reconciliation is just not worth it.

In working several years ago with two siblings in conflict, I saw that the brother was ready to spend time improving the relationship. The sister, however, was hesitant. She knew that to spend time trying to reconcile their relationship would involve not only a discussion about how she had been hurt, but about who she was and how she felt unappreciated. These were tough subjects, and her dilemma was to either work through the feelings alone (and/or keep them buried), or spend time in some sense reliving the pain of her feelings as she revealed herself to her brother. That does not sound like much fun, but they both knew, down deep, that reconciliation was important to their own mental and spiritual well-being, in addition to the well-being of the broader family.

Questions for Reflection and Discussion:

As you look at conflicts throughout the world, or in your life, what do you think are some of the main obstacles to reconciliation?

Do you know of a situation where someone should reconcile with a family member but can't bring themselves to do it? What do you think prevents them from doing so?

Have you ever experienced what you would call genuine reconciliation with another person?

✐ Reflection Two: The Desire and the Opportunity to be Reconciled

Joseph's singular question about his father suggests a desire to be reintegrated into the family. And from Jacob's standpoint, his love for, and desire to be connected with, his sons is a major theme throughout our reading.

As I've watched family business members struggle through conflict, I sense in almost everyone a desire to be connected, to be reintegrated, to become a part of the family system once more despite the annoyances, frustration and pain. Their estrangement leaves them missing one another, and to be connected would restore the relationship. It would fill a void.

When you consider that your family business consists first of family members, connected biologically and emotionally over decades, this desire for re-connection is natural and powerful. Despite abuse and violence, family members, down deep, long to be in relationship with one another. I once told two brothers in conflict that no matter how big they built their businesses, or how much wealth they passed on to their kids, on their deathbed they would regret not having reconciled their relationship. I knew I was onto something true because I was promptly asked to leave!— and I interpreted this to mean the family wasn't yet ready to reconcile.

Sometimes, the opportunity you may have as a family member is to create the space for other family members to reconcile. Joseph's brothers being back in Pharaoh's house created the physical opportunity for reconciliation. A good friend and client did just that in his family business several years ago. When conflict shook the family relationships, and after some time elapsed, he looked for opportunities to put the parties in proximity to one another. While he could not compel them to reconcile, the act of encouraging them to spend time together helped nudge the conflict toward resolution.

So in your consideration of what it means to reconcile, I encourage you to think more broadly about your role. Sometimes you may need to initiate reconciliation with someone you've hurt or be open to reconciling with someone who has hurt you. And sometimes you have a chance to encourage reconciliation among family members at odds. Either way, the family that reconciles builds stronger bonds and thus a stronger legacy.

Questions for Reflection and Discussion:

Is there someone in your family business with whom you are missing a connection - someone with whom you need to reconcile?

As you consider other family members, is there a possibility you could nudge others toward reconciliation?

Chapter Eleven

Blessing the Children
(Gen. 49:1, 22-24, 28)

"Then Jacob called his sons, and said: 'Gather around, that I may tell you what will happen to you in days to come...Joseph is a fruitful bough, a fruitful bough by a spring; his branches run over the wall. The archers fiercely attacked him; they shot at him and pressed him hard. Yet his bow remained taut...' All these are the twelve tribes of Israel, and this is what their father said to them when he blessed them, blessing each one of them with a suitable blessing."

JACOB, THE FATHER of the family of promise, is about to die. Before he dies, however, he wants to leave something to his sons, not so much in the form of tangible or intangible property but in the form of words—a blessing. But his words are not those of a doddering old man feebly doling out candy to the next generation. They are, in the language of the text quoted above, words that are "suitable" to each individual son. In the literal language of the Hebrew, Jacob blessed each son "according to his blessing"— i.e., according to words that were appropriate or fitting for the particular child.

89

Thus, rather than leaving a will that says, in the old common law language, "share and share alike," Jacob will give each son his own particular blessing, paying close attention to the character and life of each son. But when we realize that the blessings are individually-tailored, we are brought into an unexpected reality of the blessing—they aren't all "positive thinking" or "upbeat" final words. Thus, these two ideas, the individuality and the irony of the blessing, are our focus.

Individuality

Joseph has twelve sons. Each son is successively named in the first 27 verses of this chapter. Some of them receive a one-verse notice; two of them receive five verses each (Joseph and Judah). Some of them will be praised for their military prowess; one will be blessed because of his rich food ("Asher's food shall be rich, and he shall provide royal delicacies"—v. 20)! We would expect, given Jacob's favoring of Joseph that Joseph would receive the lion's share of the blessing. And, indeed, the word "blessing" is used six times in the verses describing Joseph's blessing (22-26).

But, what is most astonishing is that Joseph has to cede first place in the scheme of blessing to another brother: Judah. Judah will be the one from whom "the scepter shall not depart" (v. 10), the one through whom comes the line of Christ. Maybe the long time without Joseph in the family home made Jacob truly begin to appreciate the specialness of another child.

Irony

Almost completely unexpected in the list of blessings are negative words that Jacob leaves for some of his sons. We know, for example, that the oldest, Reuben, violated his father's trust by sleeping with his father's concubine Bilhah (Gen. 35:22). No comment is made in the text when it happened, other than that

Jacob "heard" of it. But now, the blessing becomes a time for fatherly instruction or even retaliation.

Though he recognizes Reuben's rank and power, he says, bluntly, "Unstable as water, you shall no longer excel, because you went up onto your father's bed; then you defiled it" (v. 4). This is deathbed tough love, a kind of grim recognition that crucial decisions you make in life define your future.

And it continues. Simeon and Levi, brothers two and three, had deceptively sowed bad blood with neighbors by betraying them and killing all the males in a village (Gen. 33). Because of this act of violence, their "blessing" would be that they are "divided" in Israel, never getting a tribal allotment of land. They were hotheaded men, and the "blessing" turns into a "curse" for them. "Cursed be their anger, for it is fierce" (v. 7). Perhaps our ultimate destiny is to become what we actually are.

Much more could be said of the blessings, but let's leave it here with its specificity, its unexpected character, its irony, and its somewhat brutal realism. It is as realistic as life itself.

Reflection and Questions

✑ Reflection: The Importance of "Gathering Around"

The very first words in this passage offer one of the most important lessons in the world of families and family businesses: that of meeting together to discuss the future. Too many families are either uncomfortable or fearful of having a discussion about what will happen in "the days to come." We are never told if Jacob worried that he might offend some of his sons with his negative words, but the result is that all of the sons knew where they stood with Jacob. Such a result – knowing exactly where you stand with others – is all too often missing in today's family business.

Why is it that families and family business members have trouble communicating about the future? There are at least four reasons why I think this is difficult or, in other words, four hurdles to overcome before families can usefully talk about the future together.

First, in a family business there can be significant complexity in figuring out the future. Crafting a plan for the transition of assets in light of tax laws and legal entity structures, feeling confident about range of management skills necessary to lead the business through its next phase, all while providing for financial security of the retiring generation, can seem quite overwhelming. Accountants, attorneys, wealth managers, consultants, insurance representatives…where and with whom to begin? Who leads? Does it ever end? The fact is there no simple paint-by-numbers approach when it comes to drawing a picture of the future. It can seem overwhelming for some, and sometimes it becomes an insurmountable hurdle.

Second, family member roles, contributions, relationships and problems are a moving target. A family I know in which many of the adult children don't get along – but are successful business owners in their own right – continually moves in and out of conflict. As the parents think through the process of telling their kids about their "blessing" (their inheritance), they sense that how the relationships look today may change. Parents don't want to take a chance that they will upset their adult children by discussing their current intentions, as talking about the transition may create expectations or disappointments that will be hard to manage. Sometimes the parents are not even in agreement about how the future should look, further complicating attempts to describe the blessing. They decide now is not the time.

Third, the act of gathering certain family members together might dredge up conflicts from the past. If a family has swept conflict under the rug, or there is a hostile environment with certain in-laws, the process of discussing the future may bring up pains of the past. It may in fact be difficult to gather people in a room because of unresolved tension. In short, the wounds of the past might block our attempts to describe our goals for the future.

Finally, you have the issue of mortality. Describing the future suggests a time beyond the current senior generation. The more specific the blessing, the more difficult it may be for a father or mother to deal with the fact they won't live forever. And while we know of our mortality on a general level, thinking about it in ways that are specific to a family member can sometimes be too much to bear.

A number of the reasons mentioned here assume the parents initiate a conversation about blessing. Often times, the adult children don't want to offend their parents by asking what they intend to do with the business or their assets. They are uncomfortable asking what their blessing really is, or where they stand.

The net result of all of these obstacles is silence, with the parents often setting up future conflict over assets and intentions, and the kids developing unchecked expectations about the future.

After completing my master's degree, I went back to my family's farm and ranch, hoping to provide mediation services to business-owning families. A few months after my return, I met the CEO of an accounting firm, who told me of their dilemma. Their firm did significant estate tax planning for high net worth clients, saving them millions of dollars in taxes, but if the family didn't have an inclusive conversation about what would happen in the future, the accountants would instead often find themselves in the middle of a family dispute, or they would start projects but never finish them due to the client's indecision or fear of communicating the results. Their planning wasn't as effective as he thought it could be. The family conversation, he felt, needed to happen in advance of the estate planning so that the plan could effectively match the desired goals (the blessing) of the family.

Is it an easy conversation? No. Might it create some conflict? Possibly. But the future conflicts, stress and assumptions that tended to occur *without* the discussion also created significant problems. In short, having the conversation was better than the alternative, in that it could *prevent* significant future problems. Having the discussion while the parents were alive offered an opportunity to get past any conflict, create understanding, and avoid the gossip and assumptions that occur in the absence of clear communication.

Questions for Reflection and Discussion:

Has your family had a serious conversation about the future of the business or assets? What was the result?

Are there obstacles preventing your family from having such a conversation? What are they?

What emotions would come up if your family "gathered around" to discuss the future?

Could you lead a conversation about your family's future? Why or why not?

Chapter Twelve

Making Reconciliation Last
(Gen. 50:20-21)

[Joseph is speaking to his brothers] " 'Even though you intended to do harm to me, God intended it for good, in order to preserve a numerous people, as he is doing today. So have no fear; I myself will provide for you and your little ones.' In this way he reassured them, speaking kindly to them."

THE TITLES OF chapter 10 and this chapter are intended to play off each other, much like different colored lights playing simultaneously off the same surface. There can be "reconciliation *at last*," even though the reconciliation might not *last*. What is the key to making the reconciliation, which was so movingly presented in Genesis 45, "stick"? Or, to put it differently, how can the powerful emotion and the tearful reunion of Genesis 45 become the heartfelt reality once humdrum life returns? What is to prevent the brothers from returning to the old patterns of behavior and just continuing the unhealthy family drama of earlier days?

The passage just quoted teaches us two things that will help break the cycle of dysfunction that engulfed the family of Jacob. First, someone needs to put a new interpretation on the past or give a convincing way of explaining what has happened that is actually a "pro-family" explanation, rather than a corrosive one. Second, on a more practical level, they need to engage themselves in each other's family life. A word on each reason will be helpful.

The New Interpretation

Families have their histories and their drama. Families, however, don't just experience important things with each other one time; they revisit those things and talk about them again and again. When families rehearse their common history they don't do so simply to get a few laughs or have something to talk about, but in order to develop and extend a *shared understanding* of what it really means to be family. We exchange understanding in order to develop a deeper, fuller and more satisfying interpretation of the past we experienced together.

But this talk about the past is loaded with perils. It runs the risk of digging up old skeletons, reopening old wounds, picking old fights that long ago should have ended. In the case of Joseph's brothers, thinking about the past could lead them in a number of unhealthy directions: questioning brothers' motives and actions, accusing the father of infidelity and favoritism, harping on long-buried hurts.

In this case, however, Joseph gives a new interpretation of the past, an interpretation that will forever forestall their ability to look at the past as just ghosts that terrify or memories that bite. In a word, rather than blaming his brothers for actions, he places life in *theological* terms. "Even though you intended to do harm to me, God intended it for good." This sentence is one of the most powerful statements of faith in Scripture because it affirms that behind, before, on top of, under all the machinations of human agents is the overriding providence of a good God, a God who wants to preserve life, and preserve the family. Thus, whenever anyone in the future might try to reopen old wounds, a ready and convincing rebuttal stands close at hand: 'even if you meant it for evil, God, who is in charge, meant it for good.' That is now the new, and final, word.

New Family Life

But we can't leave this story without noting the final words Joseph utters, "have no fear; I myself will provide for you and your little ones." The second key to making reconciliation last is the involvement of Joseph and the brothers in each other's family life. It is one thing to reconcile with people of your own generation and those who share the common family roots, but once you go beyond that, to take an interest in, provide for, seek to know those of the next generation, you have as much as said, 'the controversies and conflicts of an earlier generation are over. I believe in the future.' The key to lasting reconciliation is to realize that the future beckons, that those who will occupy and lead that future are those smaller or younger creatures around us, and that they need to be nurtured and cared for.

Conclusion

The final word from the story of Joseph is one of hope. Before Joseph died, he expressed his desire that his bones be carried from Egypt and interred in the Holy Land (Gen. 50:25). Several hundred years later, we have this little verse tucked into the end of Joshua, "The bones of Joseph, which the Israelites had brought up from Egypt, were buried in Shechem" (Joshua 24:32). When reconciliation happens, people's final wishes are honored, and a tight circle of intimate closure can be drawn. That, indeed, is the fruit of reconciliation.

Reflection and Questions

✏ Reflection: The Theological Lens and Family Reconciliation: No Going Back

The idea that Joseph came to see that the wrongs committed by his brothers were ultimately used for good suggests a remarkable ability to reframe a negative event. In modern and secular terms, Joseph's "explanatory style" – how one looks at why an event was positive or negative – was optimistic. He experienced a negative event but did not internalize it; he didn't let it get him down, and in fact saw the event as one with a particular purpose. (Recall that we see also this perspective earlier in his life, while he was in prison.)

Not only was Joseph's recasting of the conflict helpful to moving forward, his commitment to future with his family is unwavering. When Joseph reconciles with his brothers, he doesn't go back to life as it was. He doesn't say "thanks for the meeting," sending them on their way with some coffee and donuts. On the contrary, he makes a commitment to be involved in their lives and in the lives of their children. He makes the decision to involve himself in the relationship with his current and future family. His life changes right along with those with whom he once experienced significant conflict. Similarly, the act of reconciling in a family or family business creates a new pattern of relationship. You can't restore the relationship and then go back to life as it was during, or even before, the conflict. Things do not pick up where they left off. After the conflict and reconciliation, everything is different, and it takes some getting used to.

A father I know experienced significant conflict with his son throughout high school and college. They were always frustrated with one another – so much that his son chose not to return to the business. In fact, the father and son didn't speak for many years. Later, a friend of the father encouraged the father and son to reconcile, which they did by virtue of the father reaching out to the son. The result of that reconciliation was that the son then became involved in the business.

The re-establishment of their relationship contained some awkward and uncomfortable moments, for both father and son and their family members who had grown accustomed to the conflict. But over time, new behaviors took hold and new modes of communication became commonplace. A generation later, they are working together in ways neither would have imagined two decades ago.

Similarly, a family member who had grown disenchanted with her siblings and parents after some disagreements broke off almost all communication with the family. She lived far away and it seemed she was "out of sight, out of mind." But after several years – and some interest by her kids (the third generation) in the business – she reached out and many in the family reconciled with her. As the relationships took on new forms, she became a significant presence in the parents' end-of-life care. Who would have thought that she might play such a role when earlier years had been marked by disagreements and silence?

The point is that once reconciliation happens, the relationship takes on a new form, a new pattern. In Joseph's case, as in many family business cases, that pattern has significant implications for the next generation. By reconciling you are indeed "setting the stage" for future family dynamics. You become what we saw in our first chapter, the Backstory, in effect creating the environment – the future – into which the family business transitions. Your "relationship legacy" becomes a gift to the next generation of family members and family business participants.

The idea that God wants us to be reconciled to one another is mentioned several places in the Bible; one of my favorites is:

"So if you are offering your gift at the altar and there remember

that your brother has something against you, leave your gift there before the altar and go. First be reconciled to your brother, and then come and offer your gift," (Matt. 5:23-24).

The message is that God wants us to be reconciled, to live in peace, with our brothers and sisters. Thus, the first step in making reconciliation last involves an understanding that we are fulfilling our part of God's calling. Reconciling with family is no doubt difficult, but like other choices involving our faith and choosing the sacred over the worldly, the decision can seem easier when put in the context of God's desire for us.

Questions for Reflection and Discussion

How do you view negative events, especially conflict with other family members? Are such events usually "relationship-enders" or "temporary setbacks?"

Do you find it difficult or relatively easy to put a theological interpretation on life ("God meant it for good")?

What experiences of your family or family business have been difficult for you to interpret in a theological way?

Would things have turned out differently in your family business if there had been more reconciliation among prior generations? Do you consider it a gift when those that came before you were able to work through their differences?